# Southern Keto Cookbook

Burn More Than 15 Lbs in 1 Month and Stay Healthy WithThese 40+ Quick, Easy, and Delicious Home-Made Recipes that are High Protein, High Fat, and Low Carbs, Everyone Can Follow

# Table of Contents

# Introduction

The ketogenic lifestyle needn't bother with a repentance of flavor! Various people feel that going keto suggests they need to give up American customary dishes, anyway with a little creative mind by far most of your main food assortments can be made keto. Southern Keto will disclose to you the most ideal approach to make your main comfort food sources awesome and low-carb. You don't have to stop any affectation of breading, cheesecake, burned chicken, or rolls.

3 Proven Benefits of a Ketogenic Diet

1) Keto diet prompts weight reduction. In the event that you keep away from sugars, your body starts to consume put away fat; consequently diminishing craving. Then again, you can encounter higher energy levels.

2) Mental clearness and better fixation. Our minds use ketones as the fundamental fuel in the keto diet, in this way bringing down poisons' substance. This will altogether improve your psychological capacity.

3) Health benefits. Keto diet limits sugars, unfortunate sweet food sources, and refined grains like bread, pasta, and white rice. Then again, it advances food varieties with excellent proteins (this is significant for building muscle), great fat, and solid vegetables. Numerous examinations have avowed that a low-carb diet can essentially improve wellbeing. They estimated significant outcomes like LDL cholesterol, HDL cholesterol, glucose levels, fatty oil, and weight reduction.

Such sleek fish (e.g., fish and salmon) are known for their capacity to bring down fatty substance; along these lines, stroke hazard might be lower d. Unsaturated high-fat food varieties like seeds, nuts, and crude vegetable oils can likewise help the body lower fatty oil. Additionally, diminishing starches can bring down insulin levels and control glucose levels. Keto diets can improve actual execution and increment weight reduction as well as treat genuine conditions. Keto diets have proven valuable in the treatment of different cerebrum sicknesses like epilepsy in kids. Additionally, ketogenic diets are very viable in the treatment of the metabolic condition.

# Keto southern meals 30+ recipes

## 1. Low Carb Pecan Pie (Using Gelatin)

**Prep Time: 1 Hour| Cook Time: 1 Hour |Servings: 10 Slices**

## Ingredients:
- Outside layer
- 1 Keto Pie Crust

## Filling:
- 3/4 cup unsalted margarine
- 1/2 cup erythritol
- 1 3/4 cup hefty whipping cream
- 1/2 tsp pink salt
- 15 drops fluid stevia
- 1 1/2 tsp hamburger gelatin powder
- 1 large egg, room temperature
- 1 1/2 cups crude walnuts, generally chopped

## Guidelines:

1. Preheat the oven to 350 degrees F. Prepare pie hull for 8-10 minutes and permit to cool.
2. Dissolve margarine and erythritol in a large pan over medium-low heat. Cook 6-8 minutes, mixing often, until brilliant brown.
3. Gradually add 1 ½ cups cream and bring to a stew for 15-20 minutes, until thickened and the shade of caramel.
4. Eliminate skillet from heat and mix in vanilla concentrate and stevia. Put to the side to cool. Then, blossom gelatin in leftover virus cream for 5 minutes.
5. Tenderly whisk egg in a perfect bowl. Shower ¼ cup of caramel sauce in gradually, continually racing to temper the egg. Steadily rush in excess caramel sauce, at that point sprouted gelatin.
6. Layer the lower part of the cooled hull with chopped walnuts. Pour the wet ingredients blend over top of the walnuts and outside covering every one of the walnuts.
7. Cover the outside layer edges with foil or a pie monitor so it doesn't consume. Heat for 45-55 minutes until filling is set.
8. Permit to cool for 20 minutes preceding serving. Best saved the counter as long as three days or in the refrigerator up to ten.

**Nutrition Facts:**
- Amount Per Serving
- Calories 505Calories from Fat 459

**% Daily Value\***
- Fat 51g78%
- Carbohydrates 7g2%
- Fiber 3g12%
- Protein 7g

# 2.    Low Carb Pecan Pie (Using Sugar Free Maple Syrup)

**Total Time: 3 Hours 30 Minutes| Servings: 10 Slices| Calories Per Serving: 259.2kcal| Prep Time: 25 Mins| Cook Time: 1 Hour 5 Minutes**

**Ingredients:**
- Outside
- 1 Keto Pie Crust

**Filling:**
- 2 Large eggs
- 10 Tbsp. erythritol
- 2 Tbsp. Butter
- 10 Tbsp. sugar free maple syrup
- 1 Tsp vanilla concentrate
- 1 1/2 Cups Raw Pecans generally chopped

**Directions:**

1. Preheat the oven to 350 degrees F. Prepare pie outside layer for 8-10 minutes and permit to cool.
2. Add every one of the ingredients, with the exception of the walnuts, into a blending bowl and join well.
3. Layer the lower part of the cooled hull with the 1/2 cups of generally chopped walnuts.
4. Pour the wet ingredients blend over top of the walnuts and hull covering every one of the walnuts.
5. Spot pie into a 350 degree oven for 50 minutes.
6. When you haul the pie out of the oven let it set several hours prior to cutting into it!
7. Serve at room temperature or reheat after it is completely set and enjoy!

**Nutrition Facts:**
- Amount Per Serving
- Calories 259.2Calories from Fat 225

**% Daily Value***
- Fat 25g38%
- Carbohydrates 9.3g3%
- Fiber 4.9g20%
- Protein 4.65g

# 3. Low Carb and Keto Friendly Southern Butter Cake Recipe

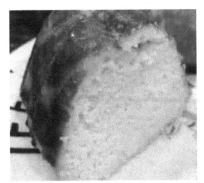

**Prep Time: 10 mins| Cook Time: 45 mins| Total Time: 55 mins| Servings: 16|Calories: 267 kcal**

## Ingredients

- 2.5 Cups Almond Flour
- 1 Cup Coconut Flour
- 1/4 Cup Egg White Protein
- 1 Tbsp. Baking Powder
- 1/2 Tsp Salt
- 1 Cup Salted Butter Softened
- 1 Cup Swerve I utilized the granular variant
- 7 large eggs
- 3 tsp vanilla concentrate
- 1/2 cup Heavy Whipping Cream
- 1 Cup Water

**Optional**
**Butter Cake Topping thoughts:**
- Sprinkle Powdered Swerve on top or top is with a low carb cream cheese frosting as found in this Low Carb Lemon Pound Cake formula we shared a couple of months prior.

Guidelines
- In the first place, start by joining the mellowed margarine and Swerve sugar along with a blender until it is very much consolidated.
- Then, add the wet ingredients to the margarine combination.
- At long last, add the excess dry ingredients to the margarine combination and mix.
- The player will come out fairly thick and spreadable. This is great!
- Shower a Bundt skillet with non-stick cooking splash and afterward dust totally with coconut flour. Make certain to cover the Bundt container totally to abstain from staying.
- Heat it at 350 degrees for around 45 to 50 minutes until its brilliant brown. Do the toothpick test importances place a toothpick in the cake and on the off chance that it confesses all, it's finished?
- You can make this as a sheet cake however the cooking time will be much less. It might just take it around 20 to 25 minutes at 350 degrees.

**Nutrition**
- Serving: 1slice
- Calories: 267kcal
- Carbohydrates: 7.1g
- Protein: 8.2g
- Fat: 25g
- Cholesterol: 120.3mg
- Sodium: 218mg
- Fiber: 1.9g
- Sugar: 1g

# 4. Low Carb Smoky Bbq Ribs

**Prep Time: 10 mins| Cook Time: 8 hr. 10 mins| Total Time: 8 hr. 20 mins| Servings: 3**

## Ingredients

- 1.1kg rack spare ribs (38 oz.)
- Without sugar BBQ Sauce
- 1/2 cup squashed tomatoes
- 1 tbsp. Worcestershire sauce
- 1 tbsp. smoked paprika
- 1 tbsp. fluid smoke
- 1/2 tsp cayenne pepper
- 1/2 tsp salt
- 1/2 tsp dark pepper
- 2 cloves garlic
- 1/4 tsp stevia powder

## Directions:

1. Mince the garlic cloves. In a bowl consolidate the BBQ sauce ingredients and blend well.
2. Spot the rack of ribs into a sluggish cooker and pour the BBQ sauce all finished.
3. Put the sluggish cooker on low and cook for 8 hours or on high for 4 hours.
4. When cooked, preheat the oven to 210C/410F. Cautiously take out the rack of ribs from the lethargic cooker (the bones will tumble off effectively) and place on a heating plate.
Spoon half of the BBQ sauce from the lethargic cooker and pour over the ribs.
Prepare in the oven for an extra 10 minutes to get that fresh flavorful skin.
5. Take the rest of the BBQ sauce and put it in a bowl. You can utilize it later to dunk the ribs in.
6. Cut the ribs up and they are prepared to serve!!

**Nutrition Facts**
- Amount Per Serving (1 serving)
- Calories 804Calories from Fat 566

**% Daily Value***
- Fat 62.94g97%
- Saturated Fat 23.81g149%
- Polyunsaturated Fat 5.73g
- Monounsaturated Fat 27.22g
- Cholesterol 208mg69%
- Sodium 771mg34%
- Potassium 699mg20%
- Carbohydrates 4.33g1%
- Fiber 0.7g3%

# 5.   Shrimp and Grits

**Servings: 5 servings| Total Time: 45 mins**

## Ingredients

### For the Shrimp:

- 1 tbsp. Tony Chachere's Original Creole Seasoning
- Spot of Salt
- 2 tsp Paprika
- 1 lb. large shrimp stripped and deveined
- 4 cuts bacon
- 1 tbsp. margarine
- 1/2 tbsp. garlic minced
- 1/2 ringer pepper chopped

### For the Sauce:
- 1/2 cup low sodium chicken or vegetable stock
- 1 tsp Worcestershire sauce
- 2 tbsp. cream cheddar
- 1-2 tsp Tabasco Sauce optional
- 1/4 cup Heavy Cream

**For the Cauliflower 'Corn meal':**
- 1/2 cup Unsweetened Almond Milk
- 1/4 cup Heavy Cream
- 2 tbsp. tomato paste
- 2 tbsp. margarine
- 1 cup sharp cheddar shredded
- 4 cups finely riced cauliflower
- 2 green onions cut (optional)
- 2 tbsp. disintegrated goat cheddar optional

## Guidelines

- In a little bowl, consolidate the Creole flavoring, salt, and paprika – at that point throw the shrimp in this blend ensuring that all the shrimp is very much covered, at that point put it in a safe spot.
- In a large skillet cook the bacon over medium-high heat, until fresh, at that point eliminate it from the container, disintegrate it, and put in a safe spot. Hold around 1 tbsp. worth of the bacon drippings in the skillet – in addition to every one of the little brown pieces in the container. You don't need to be definite with the 1 tbsp. – simply your best gauge will be fine.
- To the skillet, add 1 tbsp. of spread and the minced garlic, cook for around 30 seconds, at that point add the chopped peppers to the skillet.
- When the peppers are simply starting to mollify (around 1-2 minutes) add the shrimp. Cook until shrimp are done (around 4-5

minutes relying upon the size of your shrimp) – being mindful so as not to overcook them.

- Eliminate the shrimp and peppers from the container and put them in a safe spot. Leave all the leftover fluid in the skillet.

**For the Sauce:**
- Add the entirety of the ingredients for the sauce to the skillet. Speed until everything is all around joined and bring to a stew. Permit it to stew until it has decreased by around 1/4

**For the Cauliflower 'Corn meal':**
- In a large pan, heat the almond milk, weighty cream, tomato paste and spread until it arrives at a low bubble. Eliminate from heat and mix in cheddar. Keep mixing until the cheddar is totally dissolved.
- Mix in riced cauliflower and get back to low heat, stewing until cauliflower is done however you would prefer – blending much of the time.
- Serve the corn meal, finished off with the shrimp, a shower (or a greater amount of) the sauce, disintegrated bacon, green onions and disintegrated goat cheddar whenever wanted.

**Nutrition**

- Calories: 415kcal
- Carbohydrates: 8g
- Protein: 31g
- Fat: 26g
- Saturated Fat: 18g
- Cholesterol: 321mg
- Sodium: 1216mg
- Potassium: 699mg
- Fiber: 3g
- Sugar: 4g
- Vitamin A: 2205IU
- Vitamin C: 83.7mg
- Calcium: 378mg
- Iron: 3.3mg

# 6.    Keto Caviar Deviled Eggs

## Ingredients
- 4-eggs
- 2-tablespoons of fresh cream
- 1/2 teaspoon paprika
- A pinch of salt
- 30 g of caviar
- 1-sprig of fresh dill

## Directions
1. Boil the eggs. Fill a pan with water, add the eggs, and put them on the stove. When it starts to boil, count 5 minutes and put it away from heat.
2. Cool them with water, then dispose of them carefully to maintain the egg's dazzling look.

3. Take a knife and cut the eggs in half. Using a spoon, remove the yolk from the inside and make sure that the white part does not break. Place all bears in a separate container.  Add the sparkling cream and paprika to the yolks. Mix well until a thin, clean cream is made.
4. Place the halves of the eggs on a plate. Fill the inside with the aggregate you made with the yolks. Cover with the sturgeon eggs you chose at the peak of the combination.
5. Sprinkle with a few peppers to give it a pop of color. Then put some dill leaves on top of the combination and after the caviar.

**Nutritional Value**
- Calories: 106 kcal
- Carbohydrates: 3 g
- Protein: 7 g
- Fat: 6 g
- Saturated fat: 2 g
- Cholesterol: 215 mg
- Sodium: 301 mg
- Potassium: 80 mg
- Fiber: 0 g
- Sugar: 1 g
- Vitamin A: 335 IE
- Calcium: 39 mg
- Iron: 1.2 mg

# 7. Southern Easily Cooked Cabbage

## Ingredients

- Half cabbage
- 6-cloves of garlic
- ½ chili pepper
- 60 ml extra virgin olive oil
- Salt and pepper

## Directions

1. Wash and cut the cabbage into batches, first 1/2, then every 1/2 into smaller pieces. Add a liter and 1/2 water in a frying pan, a little salt, and a bay leaf. Upload the cabbage when the water is boiling. Boil for 8 minutes, then drain and store.
2. Cut the garlic cloves into large chunks and the chili, add virgin olive oil to a non-stick frying pan.

3. Fry the garlic for 2 to 3 minutes so that they turn brown when burned. Then remove the garlic from the pan; go away with the chili, however. Now add the well-drained cabbage and simmer for 7-10 minutes. Add salt and pepper and let stand for a few minutes before serving.

# 8.  Frijoles Negros (Cuban Black Beans)

## Ingredients:

- 
- 450 grams of black beans
- 10-cups of water (2,400 milliliters)
- 6-tablespoons of olive oil
- 1-unit large onion
- 5-cloves of garlic
- ¼ tablespoon of oregano dessert
- 1-bay leaf
- ¼ tablespoon of ground cumin dessert
- 1-pinch of salt
- 1-pinch of pepper
- 1-tablespoon of vinegar
- 1-tablespoon of dry wine
- 1-tablespoon of sugar

## Directions

1. 1-unit large green chili Steps to follow to make this recipe:
2. To start with our Cuban bean recipes, the most important thing we will do is washing the seeds properly and soaks them with water and a bay leaf. Ideally, leave them overnight so they blow up and you can cook them better.
3. The next day, take a pan of sufficient capacity, pour in the beans with the water and bay leaf, and cook for about forty-five minutes until soft.
4. Drain when equipped and prepare the black bean stir-fry. To do this, take a deep pan and heat the olive oil. Once hot, add the chopped onion and chili, or overpowered if desired, and overpowered garlic. Remove it with a wooden spoon and fry it. Reserve a cup of the already smooth beans for later; the rest you do with the knife in the frying pan. Remove everything, upload salt and pepper to taste, oregano, cumin, sugar, and simmer for a few minutes. Do not stop stirring to prevent black beans from sticking and burning.
5. Then puree the beans you reserved in the cup, add them to the rest and let them simmer for half an hour with the pan covered. After the time, add the dry wine and vinegar, stir well and let it rest for at least 10 minutes on the fire. When they are ready to serve tablespoons of olive oil, add it and serve the Cuban's black beans, accompanied by white rice.

## Nutritional Value

- Calories: 172 kcal
- Carbohydrates: 18 g
- Protein: 6 g
- Fat: 9 g
- Saturated fat: 5 g
- Sodium: 294 mg
- Potassium: 369 mg
- Fiber: 7 g
- Sugar: 1 g
- Vitamin A: 111 IU
- Vitamin C: 9 mg
- Calcium: 23 mg
- Iron: 1 mg

# 9.   Southern Ham And Cheese Sales

## Ingredients

- 1-tube of chilled pizza crust
- 1/4 pound Black Forest deli ham thinly sliced
- 1-medium pear, thinly sliced and divided
- 1/4 cup chopped walnuts, toasted
- 2-tablespoons of crumbled blue cheese

## Directions
1. Preheat the fryer to 400 °. Roll out the pizza crust into a 12-inch on a lightly floured surface. Square, rectangular. Split into four squares. Layer ham, half the pear, walnuts, and blue cheese slices are diagonally higher than half of each square to 1/2 inch from the edges. Fold one corner to the other over the filling to form a triangle; force the edges with a fork.

2. In a greased hot air frying basket, divide the wraps into single layer batches; spritz with cooking spray. Opt for a few minutes on each roughly golden brown. Garnish with the relaxation of the slices.

## Nutritional Value
- 1-conversion: 357 calories,
- 10 g fat (2 g saturated fat),
- 16 mg cholesterol,
- 885 mg sodium,
- 55 g carbohydrates (11 g sugar, 3 g fiber),
- 15 g protein.

# 10. Ham And Cheese Empanadas

## Ingredients

- 12-cooked ham feats
- 400 g mozzarella cheese
- 12-empanada tapas
- Dried oregano
- Ground chili pepper
- 1-beaten egg

## Directions:
1. Cut the mozzarella cheese into 12 strips of about 30-35 g each.
2. Pass the bars with oregano and chili pepper and spread them in the center of each ham feta.
3. Wrap the cheese with the ham, form a bundle, and reserve. This is so that the cheese no longer explodes in the oven or during baking.
4. Stretch the empanadas' dough a little so that they are oval and place the ham and cheese applications in the center of each empanada.

5. Close the center and place a finger inward to push the ham, even if persistent in closing the sides. This is so that the ham doesn't complicate your existence the moment you create the Re-plague. Make the traditional Re-pulgue and make sure they are placed in a suitable greased baking tray with oil.
6. If desired, paint the pies, ham, and cheese with crushed egg and place in a warm oven until golden brown.
7. If you want to bake empanadas with ham and cheese, keep in mind that the oil must have a temperature of 150-160 ° C because if it had been warmer, they would have been cooked on the outside, the cheese would not be able to continue to melt. Bake them for about 3 minutes.
8. Remove the baked ham and cheese patties with a slotted spoon and place on paper towels to shed extra oil.

## Nutrition
- Calories: 415kcal
- Carbohydrates: 8g
- Protein: 31g
- Fat: 26g
- Cholesterol: 321mg
- Sodium: 1216mg
- Fiber: 3g
- Sugar: 4g
- Vitamin A: 2205IU
- Vitamin C: 83.7mg
- Calcium: 378mg
- Iron: 3.3mg

# 11. Soul Food Collard Greens

**Prep time: 30 min| Servings: 5**

## Ingredients

- 1 tablespoon olive oil
- 1 little white onion finely diced
- 3 cloves garlic minced
- 3 cups chicken stock
- 1 teaspoon red pepper drops
- 1 large smoked turkey leg completely cooked
- 32 oz. collard greens altogether washed and cut into strips.
- salt and pepper
- hot sauce

## Directions

1. In a large profound skillet or pot, heat olive oil on medium heat.
2. Include onions and cook until delicate.
3. Mix in garlic and cook until fragrant.

4. Add chicken stock, red pepper pieces and smoked turkey.
5. Heat to the point of boiling and diminish heat.
6. Cover and bubble daintily for around 20-30 minutes.
7. Eliminate turkey leg and let cool.
8. Eliminate meat from bone and cut into scaled down pieces.
9. Return meat and skin back to the pot.
10. Stew for 10 minutes.
11. Add collard greens to pot, pushing them down if necessary.
12. At the point when greens start to shrink down, cover and stew for as long as an hour or until your ideal surface is reached, mixing sometimes.
13. Add salt and pepper whenever wanted.
14. Plate the greens and pour on a couple of drops of hot sauce.
15. Serve hot.

**Nutrition**
- Calories: 415kcal
- Carbohydrates: 8g
- Protein: 31g
- Fat: 26g
- Saturated Fat: 18g
- Cholesterol: 321mg
- Sodium: 1216mg
- Potassium: 699mg
- Fiber: 3g
- Sugar: 4g
- Vitamin A: 2205IU
- Vitamin C: 83.7mg

# 12.  Southern Vegan Pumpkin Spice Frappuccino

## Ingredients

- 4 tsp instant coffee grains
- 2/3 cup canned pure pumpkin
- 1 1/2 teaspoons pumpkin pie spice
- 2/3 cup of unsweetened vanilla almond milk
- 2/3 cup of lite coconut milk from the can
- 2 tsp maple syrup or to taste
- 1-teaspoon vanilla
- 2 cups of ice

## Toppings
- Whipped coconut cream
- Pumpkin pie spice
- Ground Graham Crackers Vegan and Gluten-Free

## Directions

1. Puree all ingredients in a blender until smooth.
2. Top with whipped coconut cream, pumpkin pie spice, and ground graham crackers, if desired.

## Nutritional Value

- Servings 2 persons
- Calories 250kcal

# 13. Keto Peppermint Mocha

## Ingredients

- 1 cup unsweetened coconut milk or almond milk (from a carton, not a can)
- 2 tbsp. heavy whipping cream
- 4 oz. blonde roast coffee (brewed)
- 3 tbsp. Swerve Confectioners
- 1-tablespoon of cocoa powder
- 1-tablespoon of Perfect Keto Chocolate MCT Oil Powder
- 1/4 teaspoon of peppermint extract or more to taste
- keto-friendly whipped cream
- keto-friendly chocolate chips

## Directions

- Combine all ingredients (I recommend using an electric whisk/milk frother) except the peppermint extract and place in a saucepan over medium heat.
- Heat the mixture to the desired temperature (it took me about two minutes to get to mine), turn off the heat, add the peppermint extract and mix again.
- Pour into a glass, top with keto-friendly whipped cream and/or chocolate chips (optional), and enjoy!

## Nutritional Value

- Portions 1
- Calories 197 kcal

# 14. Keto Peanut Butter Cookies

**Yields: 22 | Prep Time: 0 Hours 5 Mins | Total Time: 1 Hour 30 Mins**

## Ingredients

- 1/2 c. smooth unsweetened peanut butter, dissolved (in addition to additional for sprinkling)
- 1 c. coconut flour
- 1/4 c. pressed keto-accommodating brown sugar, like Swerve
- 1 tsp. unadulterated vanilla concentrate
- Squeeze legitimate salt
- 2 c. keto-accommodating dull chocolate chips, like Lily's, dissolved
- 1 tbsp. coconut oil

## Directions

1. In a medium bowl, join peanut butter, coconut flour, sugar, vanilla, and salt. Mix until smooth.
2. Line a preparing sheet with material paper. Using a little treat scoop, structure combination into adjusts then press down gently to straighten somewhat and place on preparing sheet. Freeze until firm, around 60 minutes.
3. In a medium bowl, whisk together softened chocolate and coconut oil.
4. Using a fork, dunk peanut butter adjusts in chocolate until completely covered at that point get back to heating sheet. Sprinkle with more peanut butter at that point freeze until chocolate sets, around 10 minutes.
5. Serve cold. Store any extras in the cooler.

## Nutrition (per serving):
- 100 calories
- 2 g protein
- 6g carbohydrates
- 1 g fiber
- 0 g sugar, 13 g
- fat, 8 g
- saturated fat
- 20 mg sodium

# 15. Keto Cornbread Muffins

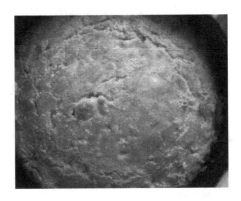

**Yield: 12 Servings | Prep Time: 10 Minutes |Cook Time: 13 Minutes | Total Time: 23 Minutes**

## Ingredients

- 1.25 cups almond flour
- 3/4 cup shredded cheddar
- 4 tablespoons margarine, softened
- 1 teaspoon heating powder
- 1/3 teaspoon salt
- 3 eggs

## Directions
1. Preheat oven to 400 degrees. In the event that using a cast iron skillet, place the all-around prepared skillet in the oven while it heats up and eliminate when the oven is at temperature. In the case of making biscuits,

similar to a biscuit dish with 8 liners, splashed with cooking shower.
2. Join the dry ingredients in an enormous bowl.
3. Add the wet ingredients to the bowl and speed until consolidated. It is alright if there are bumps.
4. Add the player to either the hot skillet or the biscuit tins.
5. For skillet cornbread, heat for 15 to 20 minutes or until brilliant brown. For biscuits, prepare for 13 to 15 minutes or until brilliant brown.
6. Store in a sealed shut compartment as long as multi week.

## Nutrition information:
- Yield: 12
- Serving Size: 1 Muffin

## Amount per Serving:
- Calories: 150
- Total Fat: 13.4g
- Carbohydrates: 2.4g
- Fiber: 1.3g
- Protein: 5.8g

# 16.  Low Carb Biscuits Recipe (Keto Friendly)

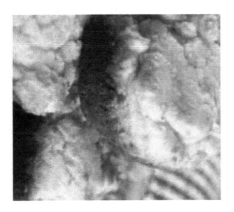

**Prep Time: 5 mins| Cook Time: 10 mins| Total Time: 15 mins | Servings: 12**

**Ingredients**
- 1/2 Cups Almond Flour
- 1/4 Teaspoons Salt
- 1 Tablespoon Baking Powder
- 1/2 Teaspoon Garlic Powder
- 1/2 Teaspoon Onion Powder
- 2 Eggs
- 1/2 Cup Sour Cream
- 4 Tablespoons Butter liquefied
- 1/2 Cup Shredded Cheese

**Guidelines**
1. Preheat the oven to 450 degrees.
2. Combine all the dry fixing as one first.
3. Join every one of the wet ingredients next.
4. Blend well.

5. Splash your container with non-stick cooking shower. I utilized a biscuit tin yet you can utilize any skillet you pick. Take a drop and drop a touch of bread roll player on your container. I likewise splash my spoon with non-stick cooking shower in light of the fact that the mixture will slide directly off into the dish.
6. Cook for around 10 to 13 minutes.

**Nutrition**
- Serving: 1biscuit
- Calories: 164kcal
- Carbohydrates: 4.6g
- Protein: 5.9g
- Fat: 14.6g
- Cholesterol: 49.2mg
- Sodium: 99.5mg
- Fiber: 1.6g
- Sugar: 0.6g

# 17. Low-Carb Sausage Gravy

**Prep Time 5 minutes | Cook Time 15 minutes | Total Time 20 minutes | Servings 8**

## Ingredients

- Pound ground breakfast sausage (not in joins) ideally fed
- 1/2 teaspoon thickener
- 1 tablespoon new sage leaves
- 1/8 teaspoon red pepper pieces
- 1 cup chicken stock low-sodium
- 2 cups weighty cream best grass-took care of
- 1/2 teaspoon ocean salt
- 1/2 teaspoon dark pepper newly ground

## Guidelines

1. Heat an enormous skillet over medium high heat. At the point when skillet is hot, add the wiener, breaking into little pieces with a spoon.

2. Cook hotdog over medium high heat until brown and cooked through. Channel off overabundance fat.
3. Spot skillet with the frankfurter over medium low heat. Sprinkle thickener on top and mix in. Mix in wise and red pepper pieces.
4. Bit by bit add the chicken stock, a couple of tablespoons all at once, mixing between options.
5. Increment heat to medium and carry blend to a stew. Stew, mixing much of the time, until blend thickens to a sauce like surface.
6. Mix in the weighty cream. Carry blend to a stew, mixing regularly. Go heat to low and stew until sauce has thickened to the ideal consistency. Mix in salt and pepper. Eliminate from heat. Taste and change preparing.

**Nutritional Information:**
- Serving size: 1/8th of recipe

**Per serving:**
- Calories: 396
- Fat (g): 38
- Carbs (g): 3
- Fiber (g): 1
- Protein (g): 12
- Net carbs (g): 2

# 18. One Pot Paleo Shrimp & Sausage Jambalaya Recipe

*Prep time: 30 min| Servings: 2*

## Ingredients
- 1 Tbsp. olive oil
- 12 ounces of andouille wiener chopped into 1/4" rounds
- 1 Tbsp. ghee
- 1 medium onion diced
- 1 cup diced celery
- 1 green ringer pepper cored and diced
- 1 red chime pepper cored and diced
- 14-ounce jar of diced tomatoes including fluid
- 2 garlic cloves squeezed
- 1 tsp oregano dried
- 1 tsp thyme dried
- 1/4 tsp cayenne (discretionary – change heat as you would prefer)

- 2 Tbsp. tomato paste
- 2 cups chicken stock
- 3 cups pre-made riced cauliflower
- 2 straight leaves
- 1 tsp genuine salt
- 1 tsp ground dark pepper
- 1/4 cup green onions chopped
- 1/4 cup new parsley
- 1/2 lemon squeezed
- 1 pound medium shrimp

## Directions

1. In a huge pot, heat olive oil over medium heat. Add cut wieners and sauté until browned. Eliminate wiener and put in a safe spot.
2. Next add the ghee, onion, celery and peppers to a similar pot. Sauté for 8 to 10 minutes until the onion is clear.
3. Presently add the canned diced tomatoes, garlic, cayenne (discretionary), oregano, thyme and tomato paste to the pot and cook just until veggies and spices are mixed well.
4. Next add the 2 cups of chicken stock to the pot and heat substance to the point of boiling.
5. Presently add the chopped frankfurter you cooked, in addition to the sound leaves and salt and pepper. Heat pot back up to the point of boiling, at that point decrease the heat to a low and permit to stew for 15 minutes.
6. Next add 2 tablespoons of green onions, 2 tablespoons of parsley, lemon juice, and the shrimp. Mix well. Cover pot, eliminate from heat, and permit everything to steam together for 15 minutes – enough to cook the shrimp.

7. Eliminate cove leaves from pot.
8. Serve jambalaya over warm cauliflower rice, or the cauli- rice can be blended into the pot not long prior to serving.
9. Enhance with staying green onions and parsley.

## Nutritional Information:
- Calories: 164kcal
- Carbohydrates: 4.6g
- Protein: 5.9g
- Fat: 14.6g
- Cholesterol: 49.2mg
- Sodium: 99.5mg
- Fiber: 1.6g
- Sugar: 0.6g

# 19. Cajun Blackened Catfish

*Prep Time5 minutes| Cook Time10 minutes| Total Time15 minutes |Servings: 4*

## Ingredients

- 4-ounce or 2 (8-ounce) catfish filets
- 2 tablespoons Cajun Blackening preparing
- 2 tablespoons olive oil
- Juice of one lemon around 2 - 3 tablespoons

## Guidelines

1. Sprinkle catfish with the Cajun Blackening Seasoning.
2. Heat oil in an enormous skillet over medium-high heat.
3. At the point when the dish is hot, add the catfish and cook for around 5 minutes.
4. Turn each filet and cook for around 5 minutes more.
5. In the case of cooking bigger filets, cooking time may take somewhat more.

6. Crush lemon on the Cajun Blackened Catfish not long prior to serving.

## Nutrition

- Calories: 61kcal
- Fat: 7g

# 20.  Southern Fried Chicken Recipe (Low Carb And Gluten Free)

*Prep time; 30 min| Cook time: 20 min |*
*Servings: 6*

**Ingredients**
- 5lbs chicken leg quarters
- 1 tsp salt
- 1 tsp pepper
- 1 tsp garlic powder
- 1 tsp paprika
- 1 cup coconut flour
- oil for broiling

## Directions

1. In a huge bowl, consolidate the chicken, salt, pepper, garlic powder, and paprika. Using your hands, knead the flavors into the chicken and be certain it's all around covered. Cover and refrigerate for in any event 2 hours or overnight.

2. To plan: Add the coconut flour to the prepared chicken and throw well to cover. Heat oil around 2 inches somewhere down in a huge, weighty lined skillet (cast iron is ideal or utilize a profound fryer in the event that you have one) to 375 degrees (F). Add chicken in clusters. Try not to stuff the container or it will not get fresh. Cook for around 8 minutes for every side, or until a rich, brilliant brown.

3. Test with a meat thermometer to guarantee that the inside temperature of the meat arrives at 165 degrees. On the off chance that you don't have one, cut into a piece and ensure the meat isn't pink prior to serving.

## Approximate nutrition info per serving:

- 425 calories,
- 32g fat,
- 1g net carbs,
- 34g protein
- Cholesterol: 49.2mg
- Sodium: 99.5mg
- Fiber: 1.6g
- Sugar: 0.6g

# 21. Southern Chicken Quinoa Bowl

***Total: 30 mins | Servings: 4***

**Ingredients**

- 1 pound boneless, skinless chicken breasts, managed
- ¼ teaspoon salt
- ¼ teaspoon ground pepper
- 1 7-ounce container cooked red peppers, washed
- ¼ cup fragmented almonds
- 4 tablespoons extra-virgin olive oil, partitioned
- 1 little clove garlic, squashed
- 1 teaspoon paprika
- ½ teaspoon ground cumin
- ¼ teaspoon squashed red pepper (Optional)
- 2 cups cooked quinoa
- ¼ cup pitted Kalamata olives, chopped
- ¼ cup finely chopped red onion
- 1 cup diced cucumber
- ¼ cup disintegrated feta cheese

- 2 tablespoons finely chopped new parsley

## Directions
### Stage 1
1. Position a rack in upper third of oven; preheat grill to high. Line a rimmed heating sheet with foil.

### Stage 2
2. Sprinkle chicken with salt and pepper and spot on the readied preparing sheet. Sear, turning once, until a moment read thermometer embedded in the thickest part peruses 165 degrees F, 14 to 18 minutes. Move the chicken to a perfect cutting board and cut or shred.

### Stage 3
3. Then, place peppers, almonds, 2 tablespoons oil, garlic, paprika, cumin and squashed red pepper (if using) in a scaled down food processor. Puree until genuinely smooth.

### Stage 4
4. Join quinoa, olives, red onion and the remaining 2 tablespoons oil in a medium bowl.

### Stage 5
5. To serve, partition the quinoa blend among 4 dishes and top with equivalent measures of cucumber, the chicken and the red pepper sauce. Sprinkle with feta and parsley.

## Nutrition Facts
- Serving Size: 3 Oz.
- Chicken, 1/2 Cup
- Quinoa & 1/4 Cup Sauce

## Each per Serving:
- 519 Calories;
- Protein 34.1g;
- Carbohydrates 31.2g;
- Dietary Fiber 4.2g;
- Sugars 2.5g;
- Fat 26.9g;
- Saturated Fat 4.5g;
- Cholesterol 91.1mg;
- Vitamin A Iu 1158iu;
- Vitamin C 6.6mg;
- Folate 62.5mcg;
- Calcium 113.1mg;
- Iron 2.8mg;
- Magnesium 118.7mg;
- Potassium 685.7mg;
- Sodium 683.5mg;
- Thiamin 0.3mg.

## Exchanges:
- 1/2 Starch,
- 1 1/2 Vegetable,
- 3 1/2 Lean Protein,
- 4 Fat

# 22. Chicken & Vegetable Penne

*Active: 20 mins | Total: 30 mins | Servings: 20*

## Ingredients
¾ cup chopped pecans
1 cup daintily stuffed parsley leaves
2 cloves garlic, squashed and stripped
½ teaspoon in addition to 1/8 teaspoon salt
⅛ Teaspoon ground pepper
2 tablespoons olive oil
⅓ Cup ground Parmesan cheese
1 ½ cups shredded or cut cooked skinless chicken bosom (8 oz.)
6 ounces entire wheat penne or fusilli pasta (1 3/4 cups)
8 ounces green beans, managed and divided across (2 cups)
2 cups cauliflower florets (8 oz.)

**Directions:**

### Stage 1

1. Heat a huge pot of water to the point of boiling.

### Stage 2

2. Spot pecans in a little bowl and microwave on High until fragrant and daintily toasted, 2 to 2 1/2 minutes. (On the other hand, toast the pecans in a little dry skillet over medium-low heat, blending continually, until fragrant, 2 to 3 minutes.) Transfer to a plate and let cool. Set 1/4 cup to the side for fixing.

### Stage 3

3. Consolidate the remaining 1/2 cup pecans, parsley, garlic, salt, and pepper in a food processor. Cycle until the nuts are ground. With the engine running, steadily add oil through the feed tube. Add Parmesan and heartbeat until blended in. Scratch the pesto into a huge bowl. Add chicken.

### Stage 4

4. Then, cook pasta in the bubbling water for 4 minutes. Add green beans and cauliflower; cover and cook until the pasta is still somewhat firming (practically delicate) and the vegetables are delicate, 5 to 7 minutes more. Prior to depleting, scoop out 3/4 cup of the cooking water and mix it into the pesto-chicken combination to warm it marginally.

Channel the pasta and vegetables and add to the pesto-chicken blend. Throw to cover well. Split between 4 pasta bowls and top each presenting with 1 Tbsp. of the held pecans.

## Nutrition Facts
## Serving Size:

- 2 Cups Per Serving: 514 Calories;
- Protein 31.4g;
- Carbohydrates 43.4g;
- Dietary Fiber 8.6g;
- Sugars 4.8g;
- Fat 26.6g;
- Saturated Fat 4.2g;
- Cholesterol 53.9mg;
- Vitamin A Iu 1736.3IU;
- Vitamin C 55mg;
- Folate 127.4mcg;
- Calcium 156.1mg;
- Iron 4.6mg;
- Magnesium 138.3mg;
- Potassium 816.8mg;
- Sodium 556.6mg.

# 23. Keto Southern Eggplant Parmesan

*Active: 25 mins | Total: 1 hr. 20 mins |*
*Servings: 5*

## Ingredients

- 1 cup arranged low-sodium marinara sauce
- 4 little eggplants (around 6 inches in length; 1 3/4 pounds complete)
- 2 tablespoons extra-virgin olive oil in addition to 2 teaspoons, partitioned
- 4 ounces new mozzarella, daintily cut into 12 pieces
- ¼ cup arranged pesto
- ½ cup entire wheat panko breadcrumbs
- 2 tablespoons ground Parmesan cheese
- 1 tablespoon chopped new basil

# Directions

### Stage 1
1. Preheat oven to 375 degrees F.

### Stage 2
2. Spread sauce in a 9-by-13-inch grill safe heating dish. Make across cuts each 1/4 inch along every eggplant, cutting nearly to the base however not right through. Cautiously move the eggplants to the heating dish. Tenderly fan them to open the cuts more extensive. Shower 2 tablespoons oil over the eggplants. Fill the cuts then again with mozzarella and pesto (a few cuts may not be filled). Cover with foil.

### Stage 3
3. Prepare until the eggplants are delicate, 45 to 55 minutes.

### Stage 4
4. Join panko, Parmesan and the remaining 2 teaspoons oil in a little bowl. Eliminate the foil and sprinkle the eggplants with the breadcrumb blend.

### Stage 5
5. Increment the oven temperature to sear. Cook the eggplants on the middle rack until the garnish is brilliant brown, 2 to 4 minutes. Top with basil. Present with the sauce.

## Nutrition Facts
## Serving Size:
- 1 Eggplant & 1/4 Cup Sauce Per Serving:
- 349 Calories;
- Protein 14.4g;
- Carbohydrates 24.3g;
- Dietary Fiber 7.3g;
- Sugars 9.4g;
- Fat 22.8g;
- Saturated Fat 6.5g;
- Cholesterol 25.3mg;
- Vitamin A Iu 486.1iu;
- Vitamin C 8mg;
- Folate 46.8mcg;
- Calcium 382.2mg;
- Iron 2.2mg;
- Magnesium 43.5mg;
- Potassium 530.1mg;
- Sodium 405.1mg;
- Thiamin 0.1mg.

## Exchanges:
- 3 Fat, 3 Vegetable,
- 1 Medium-Fat Protein,
- 1/2 Starch

# 24. Pork Tenderloins with Wild Rice

***Total Time: 50 mins | Prep: 25 min| Bake: 25 min. + standing | Makes: 6 servings***

## Ingredients
- 2 pork tenderloins (1 pound each)
- 1 bundle (8.8 ounces) prepared to-serve entire grain brown and wild rice mixture
- 1-3/4 cups frozen broccoli, carrots and water chestnuts, defrosted and coarsely chopped
- 1/2 cup chopped dried apricots
- 1/2 cup minced new parsley
- 1/2 teaspoon salt
- 1/2 teaspoon garlic powder
- 1/2 teaspoon dried thyme
- 1/2 teaspoon dried sage leaves
- 1/4 teaspoon pepper

**Sauce**:
- 1 cup water
- 1 envelope pork sauce blend
- 1 tablespoon Dijon mustard
- 1/4 teaspoon dried sage leaves
- 1 tablespoon minced new parsley

**Directions**
1. Make a long way cut down the focal point of every tenderloin to inside 1/2 in. of base. Open tenderloins so they lie level; cover and smooth to 3/4-in. thickness.
2. Get ready rice as per bundle directions. In a small bowl, consolidate the rice, vegetables, apricots, parsley and flavors.
3. Eliminate covering; spread rice blend over meat. Close tenderloins; attach with kitchen string. Spot in an ungreased 15x10x1-in. preparing dish. Prepare, uncovered, at 425° for 15 minutes.
4. In the meantime, in a small pot, join the water, sauce blend, mustard and sage. Heat to the point of boiling; cook and mix for 2 minutes or until thickened. Mix in parsley.
5. Brush 2 tablespoons sauce over tenderloins. Prepare 10-15 minutes longer or until a thermometer peruses 160°. Let represent 15 minutes. Dispose of string; cut every tenderloin into 9 cuts. Present with residual sauce.

**Nutrition Facts:**
- 3 slices with 2 tablespoons gravy:
- 293 calories,
- 6g fat (2g saturated fat),
- 84mg cholesterol,
- 803mg sodium,
- 25g carbohydrate (7g sugars, 2g fiber),
- 32g protein.

# 25. Southern Roasted Chicken Thighs with Root Vegetables

*Total Time: 50 mins| Prep: 15 min + marinating | Bake: 35 min. | Makes: 6 servings*

## Ingredients
- 4 tablespoons olive oil, isolated
- 3 tablespoons stone-ground mustard
- 2 tablespoons balsamic vinaigrette
- 3/4 teaspoon fit salt, isolated
- 3/4 teaspoon newly ground pepper, isolated
- 6 bone-in chicken thighs (around 2-1/4 pounds)
- 4 medium parsnips, stripped and cut into 1/2-inch pieces
- 1 medium yam, stripped and cut into 1/2-inch pieces
- 4 shallots, chopped
- 1/4 teaspoon caraway seeds

- 4 tablespoons minced new parsley, separated
- 3 bacon strips, cooked and disintegrated, partitioned

## Directions

1. In a bowl, whisk 3 tablespoons oil, mustard, vinaigrette and 1/2 teaspoon each salt and pepper until mixed. Add chicken, going to cover. Refrigerate, covered, 6 hours or overnight.
2. Preheat oven to 425°. Spot chicken, skin side up, on portion of a lubed 15x10x1-in. preparing skillet. Spot parsnips and yam in an enormous bowl; add shallots, caraway seeds and the leftover oil, salt and pepper and throw to join. Organize in a solitary layer on leftover portion of dish.
3. Broil chicken and vegetables 20 minutes. Mix vegetables; broil chicken and vegetables until a thermometer embedded in chicken peruses 170°-175° and vegetables are delicate, 15-20 minutes longer.
4. Move vegetables to a bowl; throw with 2 tablespoons parsley and half of the bacon. Serve chicken with vegetables; sprinkle chicken with the excess parsley and bacon.

## Nutrition Facts
- 1 serving:
- 480 calories,
- 27g fat (6g saturated fat),
- 85mg cholesterol,
- 604mg sodium,
- 33g carbohydrate (10g sugars, 5g fiber).

# 26.  Southern White Pizza with Roasted Tomatoes

*Total Time: 1hr and 10 mins| Prep: 45 min. + roasting | Bake: 25 min | Makes: 8 servings.*

## Ingredients
- 4 plum tomatoes (around 1 pound), cut longwise into 1/2-inch cuts and cultivated
- 1/4 cup olive oil
- 1 teaspoon sugar
- 1/2 teaspoon salt
- Outside:
- 2 tablespoons olive oil
- 1 huge onion, finely chopped (around 1 cup)
- 2 teaspoons dried basil
- 2 teaspoons dried thyme
- 1 teaspoon dried rosemary, squashed
- 1 bundle (1/4 ounce) dynamic dry yeast
- 1 cup warm water (110° to 115°)
- 5 tablespoons sugar
- 1/4 cup olive oil
- 1-1/2 teaspoons salt

- 3-1/4 to 3-3/4 cups all-purpose flour

## Topping:
- 1 cup entire milk ricotta cheddar
- 3 garlic cloves, minced
- 1/2 teaspoon salt
- 1/2 teaspoon Italian flavoring
- 2 cups shredded part-skim mozzarella cheddar

## Directions

1. Preheat oven to 250°. In a bowl, throw tomatoes with oil, sugar and salt. Move to a lubed 15x10x1-in. heating container. Broil 2 hours or until tomatoes are delicate and somewhat withered.
2. For outside, in an enormous skillet, heat oil over medium-high heat. Add onion; cook and mix 3-4 minutes or until delicate. Mix in spices. Cool somewhat.
3. In a small bowl, break down yeast in warm water. In a huge bowl, join sugar, oil, salt, yeast combination and 1 cup flour; beat on medium speed until smooth. Mix in onion combination and enough leftover flour to shape a delicate mixture (batter will be tacky).
4. Turn batter onto a floured surface; massage until smooth and versatile, around 6-8 minutes. Spot in a lubed bowl, going once to oil the top. Cover with cling wrap and let ascend in a warm spot until practically multiplied, around 1-1/2 hours.

5. Preheat oven to 400°. Oil a 15x10x1-in. preparing container. Punch down batter; move to fit base and 1/2-in. up sides of container. Cover; let rest 10 minutes. Heat 10-12 minutes or until edges are daintily browned.
6. In a small bowl, blend ricotta cheddar, garlic, salt and Italian flavoring. Spread over covering; top with cooked tomatoes and mozzarella cheddar. Heat 12-15 minutes or until covering is brilliant and cheddar is liquefied.

## Nutrition Facts

- 1 piece: 503 calories,
- 25g fat (7g saturated fat),
- 29mg cholesterol,
- 911mg sodium,
- 54g carbohydrate (13g sugars, 3g fiber),
- 17g protein.

# 27. Southern Style Fluffy Paleo Biscuits (Keto & Low Carb)

*Prep Time: 10 mins | Cook Time: 20 mins |*
*Total Time: 30 mins | Servings: 1*

**Ingredients**
- ¾ cup almond flour
- ¼ cup coconut flour
- 1 teaspoon heating powder
- ¼ teaspoon ocean salt
- ¼ cup almond milk
- 2 tablespoons spread or ghee (Plus discretionary extra 1 tbsp. ghee or margarine to brush on top)
- 5 egg whites (Use new egg whites, not fluid whites from a container.)

## Guidelines

1. Preheat oven to 400 degrees F and line a heating sheet with material paper.
2. Alternatively, you can filter the almond and coconut flour for a significantly lighter surface. In a medium-sized bowl, combine as one almond flour, coconut flour, heating powder, salt, almond milk, and 2 tablespoons margarine. Blend ought to be coarse and brittle.
3. In a different bowl, using an electric blender beat egg whites on high velocity until delicate pinnacles structure - around 3 minutes.
4. Add the egg whites to the flour combination and mix until totally consolidated. When joining the egg whites, don't utilize a food processor or hand blender to blend as it might influence the roll surface. Utilize an electric mixer on the least setting only for a couple of moments in the event that you need to get knots out. Your egg whites will fall totally - this is normal.
5. Permit mixture to sit for five minutes as the coconut flour will ingest fluid. You need your completed mixture to be the consistency of good cereal - not very slim and not gluey. In the event that excessively slim, add coconut flour 1 tablespoon at a time and give it a couple of moments to thicken fittingly prior to adding any more.
6. Using a biscuit scoop or spoon, drop rolls onto material paper at any rate one inch separated.

7. Put in the oven and prepare. After around 10 minutes, brush the highest points of the paleo bread rolls with liquefied margarine whenever wanted. Prepare another 5-10 minutes or until the tops are brilliant brown and a toothpick confesses all.
8. It's ideal to utilize mellowed spread (not liquefied) in the batter blend.
9. Remember that fluid egg whites from the container don't froth up as pleasantly, so I suggest using new egg whites and saving the yolks for custom made mayo or keto custard.
10. The combination will be even more a thick hitter surface than mixture. Try not to be debilitating in the event that it appears to be excessively wet when contrasted with wheat-flour rolls. The player will keep structure on the heating sheet due to the egg whites. Drop onto preparing sheet and shape it how you need.
11. Any significant replacements for this formula probably will not work. The almond/coconut flour combo and the eggs are vital for the achievement of the formula. In any case, you can utilize either ghee or spread for the fat. You can likewise utilize ordinary milk or practically any kind of without dairy milk (aside from coconut milk- - it's excessively thick) instead of the almond milk.
12. Utilize whitened almond flour for the best surface. Almond supper isn't something very similar!
13. For a much lighter surface, filter the almond and coconut flour.

## Nutrition Facts

- Amount Per Serving (1 biscuit)
- Calories 175Calories from Fat 126

## % Daily Value*

- Fat 14g22%
- Saturated Fat 7g44%
- Sodium 163mg7%
- Potassium 108mg3%
- Carbohydrates 6g2%
- Fiber 3g13%
- Sugar 1g1%
- Protein 6g12%
- Calcium 73mg7%
- Iron 0.7mg4

# 28. Keto Smothered Chicken Thighs

*Prep: 10 mins | Cook: 50 mins | Total: 1 hr. | Servings: 4*

## Ingredients:
- 4 (8 ounce) skin-on, bone-in chicken thighs
- 1 teaspoon paprika
- salt and pepper to taste
- 4 cuts bacon, cut into 1/2 inch pieces
- ⅓ cup low-sodium chicken stock
- 4 ounces cut mushrooms
- ¼ cup weighty whipping cream
- 2 green onions, white and green parts isolated and cut

## Directions:

### Stage 1
1. Preheat the oven to 400 degrees F (200 degrees C).

### Stage 2

2. Season chicken thighs on all sides with paprika, salt, and pepper.

### Stage 3
3. Cook bacon in a cast iron skillet or oven-safe dish over medium-high heat until browned, 4 to 5 minutes. Eliminate from skillet and channel on a paper towel-lined plate. Channel and dispose of abundance oil from skillet.

### Stage 4
4. Return skillet to medium heat and cook chicken thighs, skin-side down, for 3 to 4 minutes. Flip chicken over and place skillet in the preheated oven.

### Stage 5
5. Heats until chicken thighs are not, at this point pink at the bone and squeezes run clear, around 30 minutes. A moment read thermometer embedded close to the bone should peruse 165 degrees F (74 degrees C). Eliminate chicken to a plate and cover with foil to keep warm. Eliminate everything except 2 tablespoons drippings from skillet.

### Stage 6
6. Return skillet to the oven over medium-high heat. Pour in chicken stock while speeding up brown pieces from the lower part of the skillet. Add mushrooms and cook until delicate, around 3 to 4 minutes. Pour in hefty whipping

cream and whisk together until daintily stewing, at that point decrease heat to medium-low. Season with salt and pepper, if important.

### Stage 7

7. Return chicken and any juices back into skillet; top with bacon and green onions. Serve promptly, spooning sauce over the chicken.
8. Keto Smothered Chicken Thighs

## Servings per Recipe: 4
- Calories: 466.3

## % Daily Value *
- Protein: 40.5g 81 %
- Carbohydrates: 2.4g 1 %
- Dietary Fiber: 0.7g 3 %
- Sugars: 0.8g
- Fat: 32g 49 %
- Saturated Fat: 11g 55 %
- Cholesterol: 158.9mg 53 %
- Vitamin A Iu: 828.1IU 17 %
- Niacin Equivalents: 17mg 131 %
- Vitamin B6: 0.4mg 22 %
- Vitamin C: 2.5mg 4 %
- Folate: 19.8mcg 5 %
- Calcium: 34.7mg 4 %
- Iron: 2.6mg 15 %
- Magnesium: 38.1mg 14 %
- Potassium: 444.8mg 13 %
- Sodium: 373mg 15 %
- Thiamin: 0.2mg 19 %
- Calories From Fat: 288

# 29. Southern Gnocchi Pomodoro

*Active: 35 mins | Total: 35 mins | Servings: 16 (2 pans)*

## Ingredients
- 3 tablespoons extra-virgin olive oil, partitioned
- 1 medium onion, finely chopped
- 2 huge cloves garlic, minced
- ¼ teaspoon squashed red pepper
- 1 ½ cups no-salt-added entire tomatoes, beat in a food processor until stout
- ¼ teaspoon salt
- 1 tablespoon spread
- ¼ cup chopped new basil
- 1 (17.5 ounce) bundle rack stable gnocchi or (12 ounce) bundle frozen cauliflower gnocchi
- Ground Parmesan cheese, for decorate

## Directions:

### Stage 1
1. Heat 2 tablespoons oil in a huge skillet over medium heat. Add onion and cook, mixing, until relaxed, around 5 minutes. Add garlic and squashed red pepper and cook until relaxed, around 1 moment. Add tomatoes and salt and bring to a stew. Diminish heat to keep up the stew and cook, mixing frequently, until thickened, around 20 minutes. Eliminate from heat and mix in spread and basil.

### Stage 2
2. In the interim, heat the remaining 1 tablespoon oil in an enormous nonstick skillet over medium-high heat. Add gnocchi and cook, blending frequently, until plumped and beginning to brown, 5 to 7 minutes. Add the gnocchi to the pureed tomatoes and mix until covered. Present with Parmesan, whenever wanted.

## Nutrition Facts
- Serving Size: 3/4 Cup Per Serving:
- 448 Calories;
- Protein 10.1g;
- Carbohydrates 69.4g;
- Dietary Fiber 4.1g;
- Sugars 5.2g;
- Fat 14.2g;
- Saturated Fat 3.3g;
- Cholesterol 7.6mg;
- Vitamin A Iu 672.9iu;

- Vitamin C 21mg;
- Folate 14.5mcg;
- Calcium 88.8mg;
- Iron 3.5mg;
- Magnesium 14.1mg;
- Potassium 229mg;
- Sodium 366.6mg;
- Thiamin 0.5mg.

**Exchanges:**
- 4 Starch, 2 1/2 Fat, 1 Vegetable

# 30. Southern Slow-Cooker Pasta

*Active: 15 mins | total: 8 hrs. 15 mins |*
*Servings: 6*12*

## Ingredients

- 2 cups chopped onions
- 1 cup chopped carrots
- 1 cup chopped celery
- 1 pound prepared Meal-Prep Sheet-Pan Chicken Thighs (see related formula), diced
- 4 cups cooked entire wheat rotini pasta
- 6 cups diminished sodium chicken stock
- 4 teaspoons dried Italian flavoring
- ¼ teaspoon salt
- 1 (15 ounce) can no-salt-added white beans, washed
- 4 cups infant spinach (half of a 5-ounce box)
- 4 tablespoons chopped new basil, isolated (Optional)
- 2 tablespoons best-quality extra-virgin olive oil
- ½ cup ground Parmigiano-Reggiano cheese

## Directions

### Stage 1

1. Spot onions, carrots and celery in an enormous sealable plastic sack. Spot cooled cooked chicken and cooked pasta together in another pack. Seal the two packs and freeze for as long as 5 days. Thaw out the packs in the fridge short-term prior to continuing.

### Stage 2

2. Move the vegetable blend to a huge lethargic cooker. Add stock, Italian flavoring and salt. Cover and cook on Low for 7 1/4 hours.

### Stage 3

3. Add beans, spinach, 2 tablespoons basil, if using, and the thawed out chicken and pasta. Cook for 45 minutes more. Scoop the soup into bowls. Shower a little oil into each bowl and top with cheese and the remaining 2 tablespoons basil, whenever wanted.

### Nutrition Facts

- Serving Size: 2 Cups Per Serving: 457 calories; protein 33.9g;
- carbohydrates 42.3g;
- dietary fiber 7.6g;
- sugars 4.4g;
- fat 18.3g;
- saturated fat 4.5g;
- cholesterol 71.7mg;
- vitamin a iu 5724.6IU;

- vitamin c 11.8mg;
- folate 93.1mcg;
- calcium 155.5mg;
- iron 4.6mg;
- magnesium 115.7mg;
- potassium 882.6mg;
- sodium 653mg;
- Thiamin 0.6mg.

**Exchanges**:
- 3 Lean-Protein,
- 2 Starch, 1 1/2 Vegetable,
- 1 Fat, 1/2 Medium-Fat Protein

# 31. Southern keto Lemon Garlic Chicken

**Total Time: 1 hr. | Prep: 20 min + marinating |
Bake: 40 min. | Makes: 6 servings**

**Ingredients**
- 1/4 cup olive oil
- 2 tablespoons lemon juice
- 3 garlic cloves, minced
- 1-1/2 teaspoons minced new thyme or 3/4 teaspoon dried thyme
- 1 teaspoon salt
- 1/2 teaspoon minced new rosemary or 1/4 teaspoon dried rosemary, squashed
- 1/4 teaspoon pepper
- 6 bone-in chicken thighs
- 6 chicken drumsticks
- 1 pound child red potatoes, split
- 1 medium lemon, cut
- 2 tablespoons minced new parsley

## Directions

1. Preheat oven to 425°. In a little bowl, whisk the initial 7 ingredients until mixed. Pour 1/4 cup marinade into an enormous bowl or shallow dish. Add chicken and go to cover. Refrigerate 30 minutes. Cover and refrigerate remaining marinade.
2. Channel chicken, disposing of any leftover marinade in bowl. Spot chicken in a 15x10x1-in. heating container; add potatoes in a solitary layer. Shower held marinade over potatoes; top with lemon cuts. Prepare until a thermometer embedded in chicken peruses 170°-175° and potatoes are delicate, 40-45 minutes. Whenever wanted, cook chicken 3-4 crawls from heat until profound brilliant brown, around 3-4 minutes. Sprinkle with parsley prior to serving.

## Nutrition Facts

- 1 chicken thigh and 1 chicken leg with 1/2 cups potatoes: 483 calories,
- 29g fat (7g saturated fat),
- 128mg cholesterol,
- 507mg sodium,
- 15g carbohydrate (1g sugars, 1g fiber),
- 39g protein.

# 32.   Healthy Southern Peach Cobbler

*Prep Time15 minutes | Cook Time1 hour 15 minutes | Refrigerate crust30 minutes | Total Time2 hours |Servings6 | Calories547kcal*

## Ingredients
## Covering
- 4 cups whitened almond flour
- 1/2 teaspoon salt
- 1/2 cup sugar or sugar
- 2 eggs
- 6 tablespoons unsalted margarine softened

## Peach Filling
- 1/2 cup unsalted margarine 1 stick
- 1/2 cup brown sugar or light brown sugar
- 1/2 cup sugar or sugar
- 1 teaspoon cinnamon
- 1/2 teaspoon nutmeg
- 1/2 new lemon, juice of about 2-3 tablespoons.

- 2 teaspoons vanilla pure concentrate, not impersonation.
- 20 oz. frozen peaches this is typically 1 enormous pack. Or then again you can join various. See notes for canned or new peaches.
- 1 teaspoon cornstarch for sans gluten, use without gluten flour.
- 1 teaspoon water
- 1 egg Beaten with 1 teaspoon of water for egg wash
- cinnamon for fixing

## Directions

1. Add the almond flour, sugar, and salt (dry ingredients) to a blending bowl. Mix to consolidate.
2. Add the eggs and dissolved spread (wet ingredients) to a different bowl and mix.
3. Add the dry ingredients to a food processor. Then, pour in the wet ingredients. Physically beat until the blend is fused. You can likewise consolidate the dry and wet ingredients in a blending bowl and blend by hand, however subsequent to testing; the best outcomes are using a food processor.
4. Eliminate the mixture and fold it up into an enormous ball. Cut the batter fifty-fifty. One half will be utilized for the base outside of the shoemaker.
5. Sprinkle a level surface with a little almond flour to keep the batter from staying. Utilize a carrying pin and carry out the mixture until level.

6. Refrigerate the batter for 30 minutes to expedite prior to dealing with. It will be truly tacky in the event that you skirt this progression. The more you refrigerate, the simpler it is to deal with. I refrigerate half of the batter after it has been carried out, my inclination. You can keep it in a ball on the off chance that you wish.
7. After you have refrigerated, cut portion of the batter into strips around 1 inch thick.

**Filling**

1. Preheat oven to 350 degrees.
2. Heat a pot or pot on medium heat and add the spread. At the point when liquefied, include the sugars, nutmeg, and cinnamon. Mix constantly. Permit the combination to cook until the sugar or sugar has softened.
3. Include the lemon juice and vanilla and mix. Pour in the peaches. Mix and permit the combination to cook for around 4-5 minutes to mollify the peaches.
4. Consolidate the cornstarch and water in a little bowl to make slurry. Mix it together and add it to the pot. Mix to completely consolidate. Permit the blend to cook for 10-12 minutes until the filling thickens and eliminate it from heat.
5. Amass and Bake
6. Splash a 8×8 preparing dish or a 9.5 inch pie skillet with cooking shower or oil.
7. Spot 1/2 of the pie outside layer into the lower part of a 8×8 heating dish.

8. Using an opened spoon, top the outside with the peaches combination. You need to utilize an opened spoon here with the goal that you don't add an excess of fluid to the shoemaker. On the off chance that you utilize an excessive amount of fluid it will be runny. I add it using an opened spoon, and afterward I finish it off with one huge spoonful of fluid from the pot.

9. Add cuts of pie covering to the top. You can organize the outside anyway you wish. In the event that you have lopsided strips, you can shape two together to frame one. Remove the rest of any strips that are excessively long. Brush the covering with the egg wash and sprinkle with cinnamon.

10. Heat for 25 minutes. Now the covering will start to brown. Open the oven and tent the dish with foil. Don't completely cover, freely tent (it shouldn't contact the shoemaker). This will keep the shoemaker from browning a lot on the top as the inside keeps on heating.

11. Prepare for an extra 20-25 minutes. You can eliminate the foil following 15 minutes if the covering needs seriously browning.

12. Important notes for recipe: You can join the pie hull ingredients by hand. It will take somewhat more and can be hard to join the ingredients to deliver a smooth covering. I discover this way works best.

13. You can substitute brown sugar or sugar for white and utilize possibly white sugar in the event that you wish.

14. Loads of individuals make peach shoemaker with a top outside layer as it were. I'm a

gigantic aficionado of the outside so I do both a base and top layer. You can slice the hull formula down the middle and do 1 layer in the event that you wish. In the event that you lessen the measure of covering utilized in this formula (and utilize 1/2 as the top layer in particular) it will bring about the accompanying macros per serving: 251 calories, 20 grams fat, 9 grams of net carbs, and 7 grams of protein.

15. Or then again you can get serious about the top layer of the outside. This will make it simpler to make a thick cross section design in the event that you are searching for that.
16. While setting the covering into the lower part of the preparing dish, I like to utilize the lower part of a glass mug to straighten it out.
17. In the event that using canned peaches I suggest 20-24oz. At times you can just discover canned in 15.5oz servings. For this situation you may select to utilize a can and a half or go with less peach. In the case of using canned, channel 1/2 of the fluid from the can prior to adding it to the pot. In the event that you utilize the entirety of the fluid the filling will turn out to be excessively soupy.
18. In the case of using new peaches, you should strip the peaches first. You may likewise need to adapt to taste. New peaches are frequently tarter and less sweet. Taste your filling over and again and add more sugar if vital.
19. In the event that you utilize locally acquired pie outside and customary sugar, the macros per serving are as per the following:

- 889 calories,
- 61 grams fat,
- 62 grams of net carbs,
- 16 grams of protein.

20. There's an enormous contrast in insight regarding vanilla concentrate versus impersonation. Vanilla will taste much better.
21. On the off chance that you utilize locally acquired pie outside layer, the heat time will be reliable. You presumably will not have to tent the skillet with foil. Utilize your judgment. In the event that the outside begins to become a brilliant shade of brown inside 30 minutes, tent it.
22. This formula incorporates margarine. You can choose if the utilization of spread is sound or not for you. You can take a stab at using oils like coconut or avocado oil in the event that you wish.

# 33. Southern bacon pizza

*Total Time | Prep/Total Time: 30 min. | Makes: 6 servings*

**Ingredients**
- 1 tube (13.8 ounces) refrigerated pizza crust
- 2 tablespoons olive oil
- 2 tablespoons grated Parmesan cheese
- 1 teaspoon garlic salt
- 1/2 cup mayonnaise
- 2 teaspoons ranch dip mix
- 4 cups shredded romaine
- 3 to 4 plum tomatoes, chopped
- 1/2 pound bacon strips, cooked and crumbled

## Directions

1. Preheat oven to 425°. Unroll and press dough onto bottom of a greased 15x10x1-in. baking pan. Brush with oil; top with cheese and garlic salt. Bake until golden brown, 15-18 minutes; cool slightly.
2. Meanwhile, mix mayonnaise and ranch dip mix. Spread over pizza crust; top with romaine, tomatoes and bacon.

3. Ramp up the flavor even more by adding torn fresh basil with the romaine.

## Nutrition Facts:

- 1 serving: 389 calories
- 23g fat (5g saturated fat)
- 16mg cholesterol
- 1236mg sodium
- 34g carbohydrate (5g sugars, 2g fiber)
- 11g protein.

# 34. Southern Pineapple Fajitas

*Total Time: 40 mins | Prep: 20 min | Cook: 20 min. | Makes: 6 servings*

## Ingredients
- 2 tablespoons coconut oil, liquefied
- 3 teaspoons bean stew powder
- 2 teaspoons ground cumin
- 1 teaspoon garlic powder
- 3/4 teaspoon genuine salt
- 1-1/2 pounds chicken tenderloins, divided the long way
- 1 enormous red or sweet onion, divided and cut (around 2 cups)
- 1 enormous sweet red pepper, cut into 1/2-inch strips
- 1 enormous green pepper, cut into 1/2-inch strips
- 1 tablespoon minced cultivated jalapeno pepper

- 2 jars (8 ounces each) unsweetened pineapple goodies, depleted
- 2 tablespoons nectar
- 2 tablespoons lime juice
- 12 corn tortillas (6 inches), warmed
- Discretionary: Pico de Gallo, acrid cream, shredded Mexican cheddar mix, cut avocado and lime wedges

## Directions

1. Preheat oven to 425°. In an enormous bowl, blend initial 5 ingredients; mix in chicken. Add onion, peppers, pineapple, nectar and lime juice; throw to join. Spread equitably in 2 lubed 15x10x1-in. heating container.
2. Broil 10 minutes, turning skillet partially through cooking. Eliminate container from oven; preheat oven.
3. Cook chicken combination, 1 container at an at once, in. from heat until vegetables are delicately browned and chicken is not, at this point pink, 3-5 minutes. Serve in tortillas, with garnishes and lime wedges as wanted.
4. In the event that you love pineapple, add considerably more as a fixing or present with an organic product salsa like peach or pineapple salsa.
5. In the event that you don't have coconut oil available, substitute with canola or vegetable oil.

## Nutrition Facts
- 2 fajitas: 359 calories,
- 8g fat (4g saturated fat),
- 56mg cholesterol,
- 372mg sodium,
- 45g carbohydrate (19g sugars, 6g fiber),
- 31g protein.

## Diabetic Exchanges:
- 3 starch,
- 3 lean meat,
- 1 fat.

# Conclusion

I would like to thank you all for choosing this book. All the recipes in this book are traditional southern easy recipes which comprise on keto diet ingredients which are very useful for people who want to lose weight. Hope you enjoy preparing delicious dishes for you and your family members. Good luck!

CPSIA information can be obtained
at www.ICGtesting.com
Printed in the USA
BVHW092057080621
609008BV00003B/402